Sitting Still
Like a Frog
Activity Book

The frog says hi!

Also by Eline Snel

Breathe Through This

Sitting Still Like a Frog

Sitting Still Like a Frog

Activity Book

75 Mindfulness Games for Kids

Eline Snel

Illustrated by **Marc Boutavant**

With five stories by **Marie-Agnès Gaudrat**

bala
kids

BOULDER 2019

BALA KIDS
An imprint of Shambhala Publications, Inc.
4720 Walnut Street
Boulder, Colorado 80301
www.shambhala.com

English translation © 2019 by Shambhala Publications, Inc.
Translated by Sherab Chödzin Kohn

Originally published under the title *Calme et attentif comme une grenouille, Ton guide de sérénité.* © Éditions des Arènes, Paris, 2017; © Audio script: Eline Snel.

9 8 7 6 5 4 3 2 1

First U.S. Edition

Printed in China

♾ This edition is printed on acid-free paper that meets
the American National Standards Institute Z39.48 Standard.

♻ Shambhala makes every effort to print on recycled paper.
For more information please visit www.shambhala.com.

Bala Kids is distributed worldwide by
Penguin Random House, Inc., and its subsidiaries.

Designed by Liz Quan

ISBN: 978-1-61180-588-8

Contents

Dear Parents,

Maybe you've already used the book *Sitting Still Like a Frog* and its CD. Many of you have seen the benefits of this method for teaching children to be attentive to each other. And now, more and more teachers are setting up the Frog program in their schools.

In this book, children will find games, activities, posters, and recipes. They'll draw, color, and read stories. The youngest ones might need your help, while older children might prefer to do the activities on their own or sometimes with you.

In our too-busy lives, spending a little quality time with our children is very precious and fun! This is not just a book of activities; it talks about inner peace, curiosity, and meditation—and it reveals the secret of happiness! It is a true guide that will accompany your little ones all through their childhood.

On the audio download web page (see below), you will find four yoga exercises, a game that teaches your child how to just listen, and the meditation of the bird of happiness.

I wish you much joy and many moments shared with the frog.

—Eline Snel

 The audio component of this book is available for download at www.shambhala.com/sittingstilllikeafrog.

stories to
meditate on

smart cards

yoga
for feeling

Hello,

I'm very happy to make your acquaintance. I created this book of inner peace for you, for children who need to know how to calm down and concentrate, for those who want to learn to be happy and love those around them, and for all those who want to make this planet a better world.

It's up to you!

activities for
learning attention

posters to
pin up

exercises
to practice

recipes to cook

pictures to create
and color

words to sing

stickers to
stick

at the end
of the book

projects and
activities

sweet words
to offer

a social game
to share

If you don't want to cut out
certain pages, like the memory
game or the wishing tree, you
can photocopy them.

The Little Girl Who Had Birds in Her Head

 THERE WAS ONCE a little girl who had everything she needed to be happy, but she wasn't. When you gave her a toy, she thought about the toy somebody had given to her brother. When you brought her some cake, she thought about the ice cream she had eaten last night.

The little girl was never completely there. She was called the little girl who had birds in her head because her thoughts flew around all the time, and she let herself be carried away by them, as though on the wings of birds.

These flying thoughts made the girl so nervous and tired that she got sick. Several doctors hurried to her bedside. But no medicine could cure her.

That's when I, the frog, decided to visit her.

The first day, I brought her a strawberry and simply said, "Taste." The second day, I told her a story, and simply said, "Listen."

The third day, the little girl was sitting on her bed. She smiled at me and asked me, "What did you bring today?" She was cured! She had discovered what it was to eat a strawberry when you eat a strawberry, and what it is to listen to a story when you're listening to a story.

From that day on, the little girl had a happy life, because she had discovered the power of attention, which gives every moment a different taste.

1
How to Train Your Attention Muscle

The frog is here—really here. It pays attention.
It doesn't let itself get distracted easily.
It sees all the agitation around it, but it doesn't react.
It remains calm and attentive, without moving.

Breathing

Most of the time you don't even realize you're breathing. With this exercise, you're going to become aware of your breath coming and going. Attention begins when you notice that you're breathing.

Put your index finger on the wavy
green lines and breathe calmly.
When the wave goes up, you breathe
air in, and when the wave goes down,
you breathe air out.

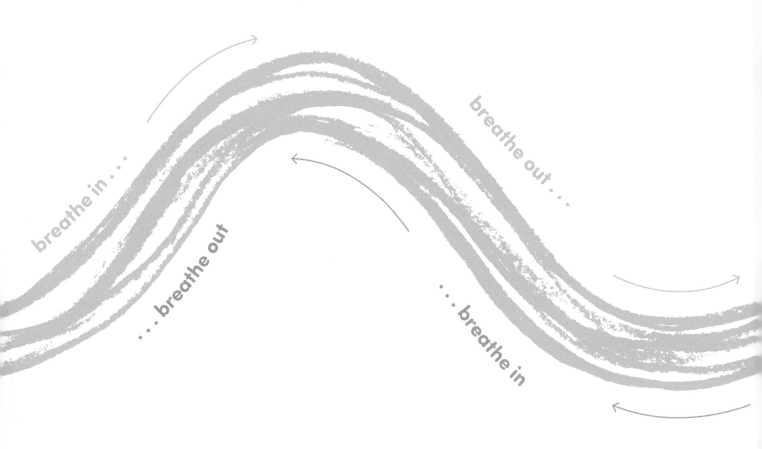

Don't try to breathe differently
than you do normally. . . .
Breathing happens
all by itself. . . .

breathe in . . . .

breathe out . . . .

. . . breathe out

. . . breathe in

At the end of the line, go back
in the opposite direction.

Drawing Your Breath

Observing your breath can be very helpful when you are angry, stressed out, or tense. Focusing on your breath will help you to calm down.

Draw the waves of your breath:

- one moment when you're upset

- one moment when you're feeling calm

- one moment when you're feeling afraid

You can't make mistakes when breathing; your breathing is always okay.

The Frog's Story:
The Lion's Fear

12

 THERE WAS ONCE a powerful and magnificent lion. In the grasslands where he lived, all the animals were afraid of him, and when he got near them, they all ran away.

I love to watch him. When he watches his prey, he is motionless, and all his senses are awake; he is the master of attention. He knows how to act without getting excited. He is alive, supple, and fearsomely efficient!

But one day, I was surprised to find this lion caught in a hunter's net. He was panicked, and he was striking out in all directions, bruising himself against the trunks of trees, tearing out his claws on rocks without any hope of freeing himself. Fear had made him lose all his skills.

At the point when he was no longer anything but a poor injured animal, I came up close to him, and I began to breathe calmly, but loud enough so he could hear my breath coming in and going out, coming in and going out.

Little by little, he began to breathe in and breathe out in the same rhythm as I did—a calm rhythm, which became calmer and calmer. Then he relaxed and looked around him. He took a look at the hunter's net, and he immediately knew what to do. With one bite, he broke through the mesh, and then, calmly tearing his prison apart with his paw, he freed himself.

He had discovered that when panic gets ahold of you, your breath is the key, and the solution will come by itself.

Super Attentive!

Here's an exercise that will require all your attention.
It has two stages: coloring, then a game.

1.

Color the first word blue,
the second green, the third red,
and the fourth yellow.

2.

Say the color of each word
without paying any attention
to what the word is. If you don't
know how to read, this will
be easy for you. But if you know
how to read, you will see that
your brain wants to say the
name of the word and not the
name of the color.

RED

YELLOW

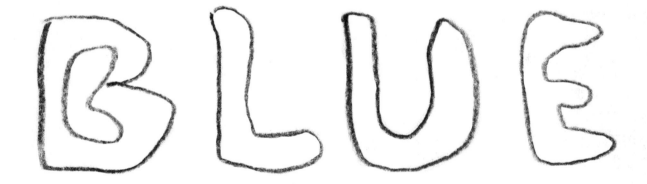

BLUE

GREEN

15

Observing

Observing with attention is an art you can learn—like music or a sport.
And by observing, you can better discover the world around you.

Look and see what line is exactly the same as the example above.

Here's a little sudoku game. Complete the two grids so that you don't have the same image more than once in any vertical or horizontal line.

Concentrating

When you observe attentively, you are concentrating.
Concentration is another word for attention.

Can you count the animals?

There's . . . a bird, . . . dragonflies,

. . . bees, . . . gnats, . . . and a snail.

Find the shadow that corresponds exactly to the frog.

Building Your Memory Muscle

In our memory there are many holes, many things that we forget.
But we can train our memory "muscle" by really paying attention.

PREPARATION OF YOUR MEMORY GAME

Cut out the cards. Write the name of what each image represents.

HOW THE GAME WORKS

For two players

1. Mix the cards up and place them face down on the table.

2. The first player turns over two cards. If they are identical, the player keeps them and turns over another two.

3. If they are not identical, the player puts them back where they were, and it's the second player's turn to turn over two cards. The player who accumulates the most pairs wins.

You can also play by yourself. The game is over when you have found all the pairs.

Do you feel the tension when you try to remember? Don't forget to breathe!

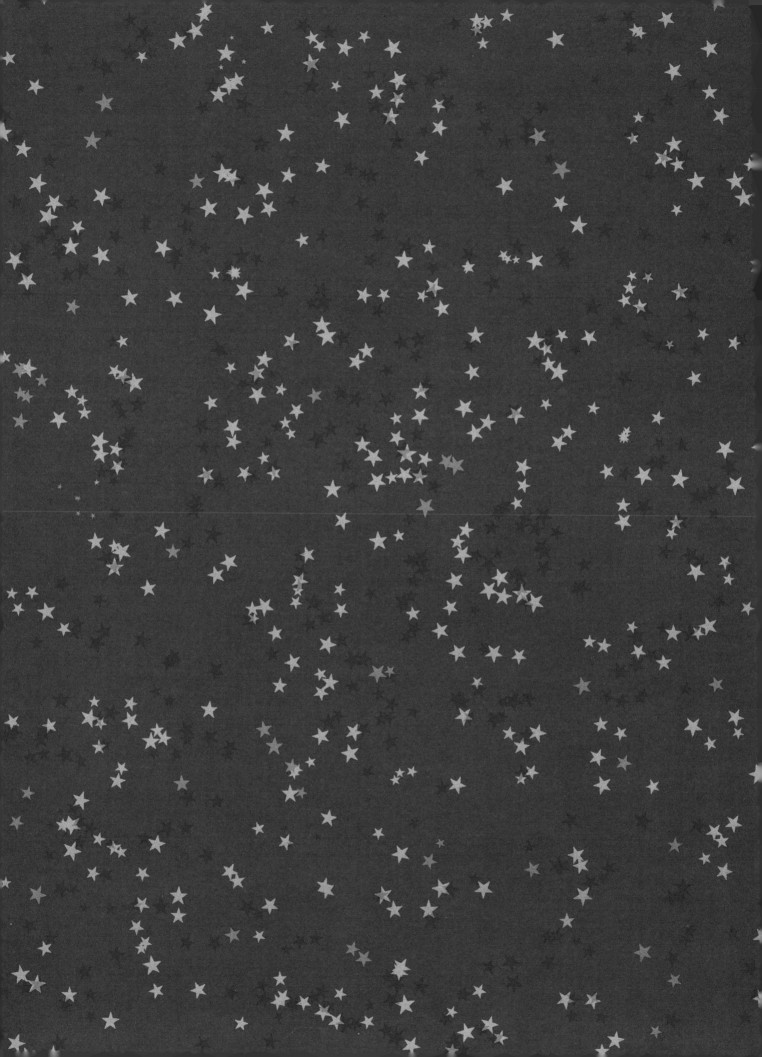

Coloring a Mandala

A mandala is a round form that you can use to help you focus, relax, or meditate. Color it in with your favorite colors. Always begin with a point in the center.

2

Your Body
Is Your
Best Friend

— Becoming aware of your body is another way to pay attention. The body is very important, but often we neglect it. We only think about it when we have a pain somewhere. Becoming more aware of your body makes it possible to feel better and see your limits—like when you are too tired or have eaten too much.

Like your breathing,
your body is always with you.
It's your best friend.

Moving Your Body

When you are doing the yoga exercises, you can also listen to your body. When you hold your breath, or when you have a little pain somewhere, your body is telling you to pay attention and slow down. It's good to listen to your body!

 BUTTERFLY YOGA

Moving like a butterfly strengthens your back and makes your hips supple.

TRACK 2

 WINDMILL YOGA

This exercise strengthens your heart and helps create balance in your body.

TRACK 1

THE KIND COBRA

TRACK 3

This exercise opens your heart and strengthens your belly muscles.

THE LITTLE BOWLS

TRACK 4

Patting your body with your hands will make you feel refreshed.

Learning to Stop

Sometimes we do things without really knowing why. We eat too much, we fight with someone, we get upset, we get overly excited. It's important to learn to stop ourselves, to take a time-out. We all have a pause button. Where is yours? When you've found it, put your hand on it and breathe calmly—and then continue to do what you were doing.

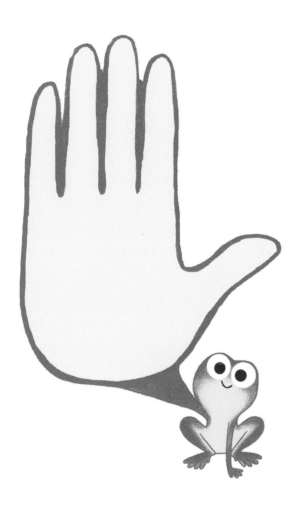

In your opinion, what situations should you use the pause button in? Check the cases below where you think it would be a good idea.

○

When you don't stop when you are asked to stop?

○

When you eat too much?

○

When you play on the computer or a phone for more than half an hour?

○

When you are very upset?

Stick the sticker
(see the end of the book)
on the place on your body where
your pause button is.

A Musical Pause

With this song, "A Little Dancing Thumb," you're going to travel to all the parts of your body.

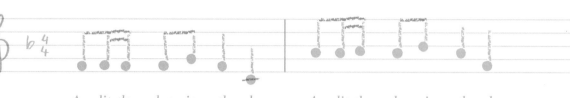

A lit-tle dan-cing thumb   A lit-tle dan-cing thumb

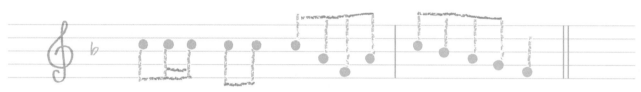

A lit-tle dan-cing thumb and that's   enough fun for me

A little dancing thumb
A little dancing thumb
A little dancing thumb
And that's enough fun for me

Two little dancing thumbs
Two little dancing thumbs
Two little dancing thumbs
And that's enough fun for me.

A little dancing finger
A little dancing finger
A little dancing finger
And that's enough fun for me.

Two little dancing fingers
Two little dancing fingers
Two little dancing fingers
And that's enough fun for me.

A little dancing hand
A little dancing hand
A little dancing hand
And that's enough fun for me.

Two little dancing hands
Two little dancing hands
Two little dancing hands
And that's enough fun for me.

Continue the song with your feet,
your legs, etc.

I feel my heart opening

and I feel myself connecting to all the humans and all the children in the world

I'm like a young tree, flexible and strong.

A lot of things can touch me, but I'm strong.

When I'm tense,
I'm like raw spaghetti.

When I'm relaxed,
I'm like properly cooked spaghetti.

I can't stop thinking, but I can stop listening to my thoughts.

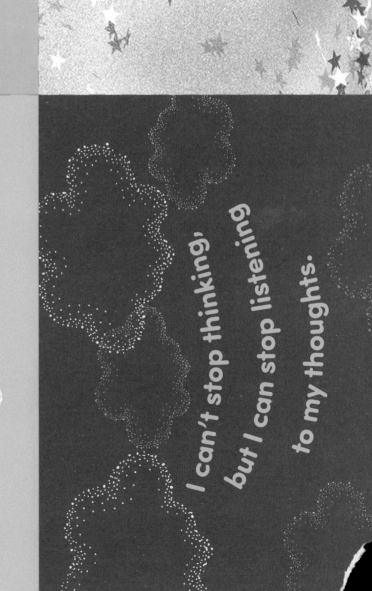

Even if I stay calm, there's always something moving in me.... It's my breath.

I want to be safe
I want to be happy . . .
with all my heart.

My attention is like a little lamp.
I can point it at the outside
or at the inside
of me.

Today
I'm paying attention to things
that make me happy.

The Heart Room

If your heart were a room, what would there be in this room? Draw what you imagine.

The Frog's Story:
The Courageous Little Boy

 THERE WAS ONCE a little boy who had a lot of courage. He got up every morning full of energy. He ran, he played, he had fun all day, and he went to bed late at night not even tired! He was sure that every day of his life would be like that.

But one morning, he woke up with a bad headache. He got up slowly and went out to get some air, groaning: "Hey, what's happening to me? It hurts, it hurts, it hurts!" And he yelled and shouted and stamped his feet, because he was afraid the pain would never stop.

That's when I came up close to him and asked, "Have you seen that daisy by your feet? Was it as beautiful yesterday?" But he didn't listen to me, and kept shouting, "Ow, ow, ow, it hurts!" It's hard to take an interest in anything else when you're in pain. So I lightly pinched his arm to get his attention, and I insisted: "Do you hear that bird singing? Was it singing the same song this morning?" He stopped moaning for a second to listen. So I got him to look up into the air by saying, "And will the clouds floating in the sky now have the same shape tomorrow?"

The little boy was quiet. He looked around him calmly. After a long moment, I asked him, "And how's your head now?" Completely amazed, he shouted, "Oh wow! It doesn't hurt anymore!!!" He smiled. He had discovered that in life everything passes, everything transforms, everything changes.

After that, the little boy resumed his normal life, with its ups and downs. But he only focused on his courage and would tell others that "When something is not going well, don't worry. Sooner or later, it will change!"

3

The Adventure of the Five Senses

You can exercise your senses
like you use your muscles—
just by being attentive.
Are you ready?

When you are a baby, you are just discovering the world, and so you really
look at things. You touch them, you listen to them, you taste them.
As you get older, you begin to think, and you always have an opinion about
everything—it's beautiful, it's ugly, it's good, it smells bad. But looking,
touching, smelling, listening, tasting all can be a real adventure.

Looking

What do you see when you really look with your eyes—
and not with your head?

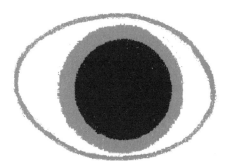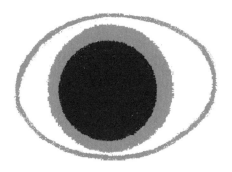

OPEN YOUR SENSES:
AN EXERCISE FOR TWO

Sit facing your dad or your mom, or one of your
brothers or sisters, or a friend.

When you look at his/her
eyes, what do you see?

What are the different
colors you see?

When you look at his/her
hair, what do you see?

Is it all one color, or are
there different colors?

And his/her mouth?
What do you see when you
smile at each other?

Is it only the mouth that
smiles, or do you see
something else?

**You really saw
each other, and that is
something special.**

. . . and Touching

ANOTHER EXERCISE FOR TWO

Take your dad's hand or your mom's hand, or the hand of one of your brothers or sisters, or a friend's hand.

Do you see the fingers? And the nails?

What do you hear when you rub your hands together?

Are they warm or cold? Smooth or rough?

What else do you see? Little wrinkles? Little cuts? A ring?

Do you feel anything else? Take the time to feel how the other person's hand looks to you.

What do you see when you really look at your hands?

Tasting with Attention

Often when you eat, you swallow fast. You don't pay attention to the taste of the food. When you cook, you become aware of all the ingredients in the recipe. And when you eat what you cooked, you discover lots of surprising tastes. Try these recipes!

Makes 4 servings

CHOCOLATE CHIP COOKIES

6 tablespoons unsalted butter, softened

$\frac{1}{3}$ cup + 1 teaspoon superfine sugar

1 teaspoon baking soda

1 teaspoon vanilla extract

1 large egg

1$\frac{1}{4}$ cups all-purpose flour

$\frac{1}{2}$ cup chocolate chips

1. Preheat the oven to 350°F.

2. In a big bowl, combine the softened butter, sugar, baking soda, vanilla extract, and egg. Mix with a wooden spoon.

3. Pour in the flour a little at a time and stir: the dough should be quite smooth. Add the chocolate chips.

4. Put a sheet of parchment paper on the baking sheet and make little piles with the dough.

5. Ask an adult to put the baking sheet in the oven for 10 minutes. As soon as the edges of the cookies begin to brown, they're done!

Something's Shaking

VANILLA MILKSHAKE

2 scoops vanilla ice cream

1 cup milk

1 tablespoon honey

BANANA MILKSHAKE

Same ingredients

+ 1 banana

STRAWBERRY MILKSHAKE

Same ingredients

+ 1 cup of strawberries

What's the texture in your mouth like?

What different flavors do you notice?

Is is cold? Sweet?

PREPARATION FOR ONE GLASS

1. Put all the ingredients in a blender.

2. Blend until you get a nice foamy milkshake.

3. Pour it into a glass. Let the tasting begin!

Smelling Smells

The world is full of smells. Most of the time, we don't notice them. Or maybe we just notice the good ones (yum!) or the bad ones (yuck!).

1. In this exercise, you are going to really use your nose for smelling, and only smelling. You're going to be like a detective who wants to know, what is it? Just smell what you are smelling at the moment, without saying "that smells good" or "that smells bad." Are you ready? Try to find as many of the items on this page as possible, and smell them!

2. What smell makes you feel good?

3. If you go out today, be attentive to the first smell that you smell.

soap

laundry

an eraser

perfume

vinegar

a garbage can

bread

an apple

a fart!

the pages
of this book

fresh air

your parents

Hooray for Massages!

Touching each other is something that we all need. Our skin is our most important sense organ. Just by being near someone, we can already feel warmth or cold, safety or threat.

GAME FOR 2: THE 5 LITTLE RASCALS

Run your fingers over your mom's or your dad's back, from top to bottom and then bottom to top. Go up and go down over and over again several times.

Then, have them do the same thing to you.

What do you feel when you get massaged like that?

waves a storm a cloud

the sun the moon a tornado

a star rain a flower

GUESSING GAME FOR 2

Draw something with your finger on
your mom's or dad's back, and ask
them to guess what it is.

After a few guesses, switch roles.

Just Listening

1. THE SOUNDS AROUND YOU

Sit down, close your eyes, and open your ears.

What sounds do you hear right now? Are they loud or soft?

Near or far? In front of you or in back of you?

Just listening is not always easy.

TRACK 5

Now you are going to hear all kinds of sounds. Can you try to listen to them as though you were hearing them for the first time, without "judging" them and without necessarily trying to recognize them?

The Sound Library

Lots of sounds exist that you have already heard or that you can imagine. . . . Now it's your turn! You can make sounds with your voice, draw them, and name them.

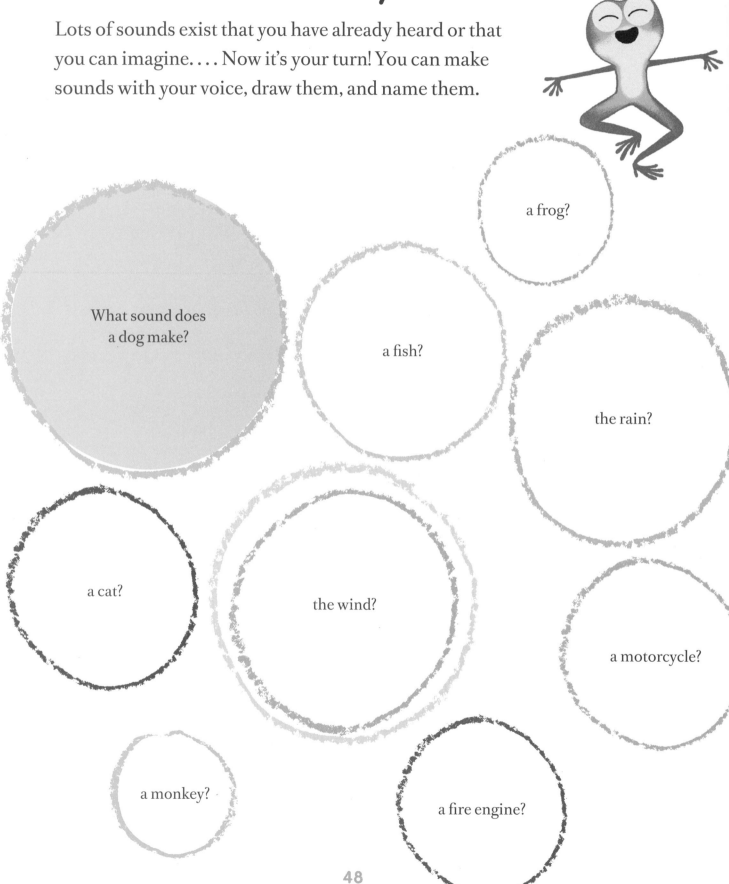

a frog?

What sound does a dog make?

a fish?

the rain?

a cat?

the wind?

a motorcycle?

a monkey?

a fire engine?

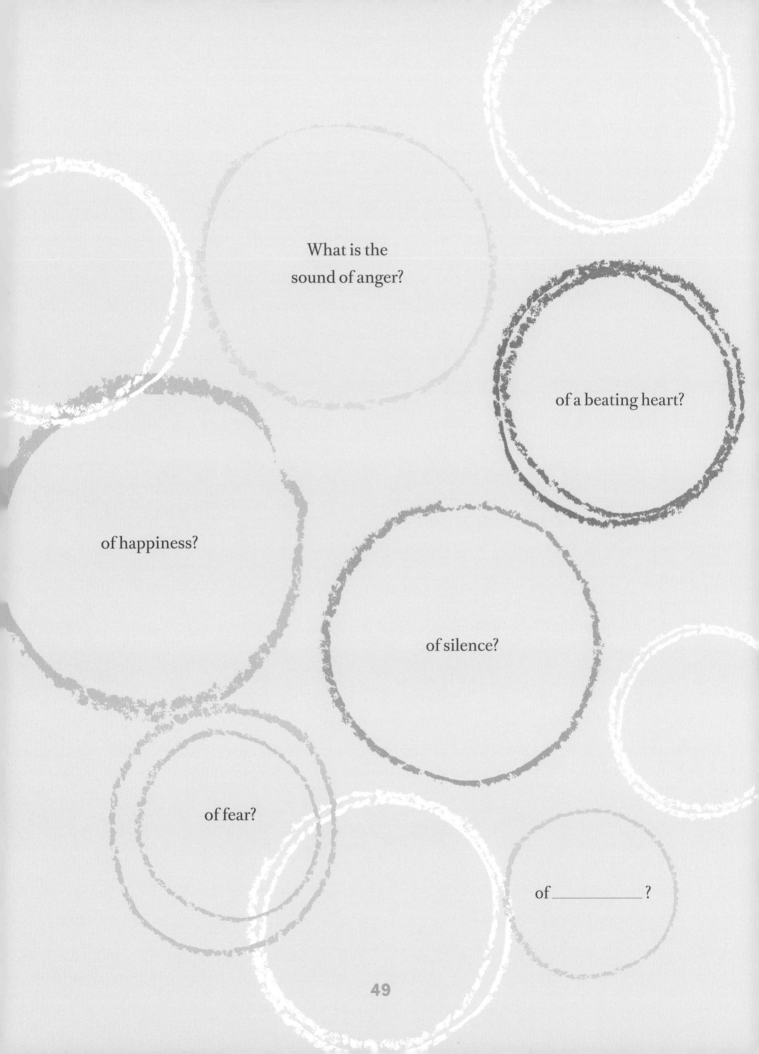

What is the
sound of anger?

of a beating heart?

of happiness?

of silence?

of fear?

of _____ ?

49

4

There's a Whole World inside You

Let's get started discovering
this vast world!

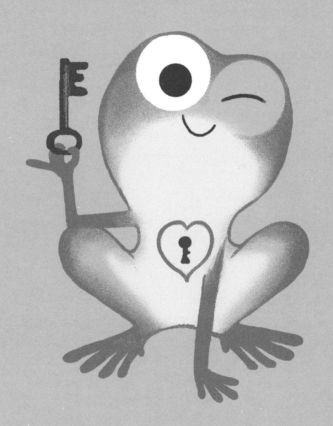

Inside you, there's a world of thoughts,
feelings, and emotions.
Sometimes you're happy, sometimes you're sad, and
sometimes you don't know what you are!
I'm going to teach you how to recognize your emotions,
how to feel them and accept them.

Your Inner Weather Report

What's the weather like inside you?
Close your eyes and observe what you feel.

What are the emotions of the different frogs drawn above?
Can you put the appropriate letter in each circle?

A. Sad   **B.** Angry   **C.** Happy   **D.** Worried

What's your inner weather
at this moment?

Draw it.

How Do You Put Out the Fire of Anger?

You have the right to be angry. For example, when you've had an argument with somebody or when your parents ask you to go to bed. Have you ever been very, very angry? Do you remember the situation? Anger can be like a little fire, so you might need a fireman to put it out.

Can you figure out which hose the frog should connect to in order to put out the anger fire? When you do, add some drops.

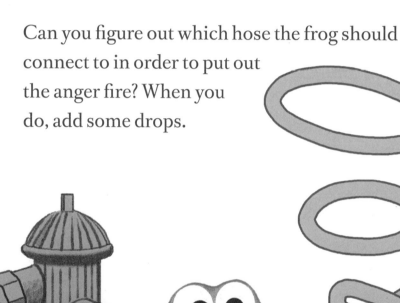

The Story of the Dandelions

 THERE WAS ONCE a king who lived in a big castle, surrounded by an enormous lawn that he was very proud of. He wanted the lawn to be a fresh green color and always cut short. He loved it like crazy and never wanted to see weeds in it or even one dandelion.

An army of gardeners took care of this lawn and primped and pampered it day and night. One morning as the king was taking a walk, he found a dandelion! It was yellow and beautiful, but he went into a fit of anger and pulled out the flower, shouting: "Throw half my gardeners in prison!"

A few days passed. Half the gardeners were pining away in prison. But one morning, the king discovered three dandelions! He went into an awful rage and shouted: "Send all my gardeners away, and bring me some who can protect my lawn!"

That's when I approached him and said, "Your Majesty, if you send away all your gardeners, the dandelions will overrun your whole lawn. In life, there are things that we don't like, and getting angry won't prevent them. They happen anyway. The only solution is to accept them. And sometimes, with time, you even get to like them."

The months passed. The dandelions bothered the king less and less. He even thought the little flowers were rather pretty. And since then, he discovered a new joy: he loves blowing the seeds off dandelions! At that moment, he liberated all the gardeners from jail.

I Love Dandelions!

Like in the king's garden, there are often dandelions in life. You too should try to accept that things are not always perfect, but are just good enough.

1. Find the seven differences between these two pictures.

2. The next time you feel upset or frustrated, plant a dandelion on this page (see the stickers at the end of the book).

The Magical World of Thoughts

Everybody has thoughts—funny thoughts, thoughts about school, thoughts about things we want or have to do, angry thoughts in the middle of an argument, kind thoughts when we want to help someone, and on and on. Wow, we never stop thinking!

1. Stick in thought stickers (see the end of the book) to imagine what is going on in these people's heads.

2. What are the thoughts that keep reoccurring in your head?

_____

_____

3. What is your favorite thought?

_____

_____

4. If you can't sleep because you think too much, put your hands on your belly and feel your breath rising and falling. A little up, a little down. In your belly, there are no thoughts!

I think about my birthday all the time.

I'm not good enough.

How to Be the Boss of Your Thoughts

Do you always have to believe what your thoughts tell you? No—some of them aren't true. They're like little stories playing in your head that prevent you from simply and clearly experiencing what you're living through. But you don't have to do what they say; you are the boss of your thoughts.

TO MAKE A MIND JAR, YOU NEED:

- a glass jar (a jam jar or any jar with a tight lid)

- 2 tablespoons liquid glycerin (available at a drugstore) to make the sequins sink slower (the glycerin will make up about one quarter of the volume)

- some distilled water (to keep it from turning yellow)

- some gold sequins (for your feelings)

- some silver sequins (for your impulses)

- red, blue, and green sequins or sequins of other colors (for all your other thoughts)

PREPARATION

- fill the jar with the distilled water and glycerin

- put in a big pinch of all three kinds of sequins and tighten the lid

1. Shake it up
2. Look at it
3. Let it settle

The Three Super Rules

MIND JAR

This soup is like your head—inside, there are all kinds of stories. And when you shake the soup, you imagine a little storm going on in your skull: everything that annoys you and all your worries start spinning around.

HOW TO USE IT

● Shake the glass jar.

● Look at the sequins swirling in the pot as in the soup of your mind.

● Wait a while for the sequins to sink to the bottom.

When you look at the sequins slowly sinking, the storm of your thoughts, your feelings, and your desires also sinks. It doesn't all disappear, but when it's all on the bottom, it doesn't really disturb you. So now you can see clearly, with a clear mind.

And then . . . you can decide how to react.

5

Be the Artist of Your Life

Have you ever noticed that, even with your eyes closed,
you see lots of things? It's unbelievable!
Anyone can make movies in their head, like a real
movie director. And the movies in your inner cinema
can help you achieve your dreams and desires.

What you dream and imagine
in your inner world can support
and help inspire you in your life.

Imagining

In school, in books, or with your parents, you learn lots of things about the outer world. But inside you, there is also a world—the world of dreams and imagination. And imagination is something very powerful that can take you very far!

1. Each of these animals has a special power. What is this power? It's up to you to decide!

2. Choose a power that can support you in your life, and imagine that you have this power in you. You can feel it, and you can look at it with your inner eye.

3. On the sticker page (see the end of the book), you will find all these animals. You can use their powers whenever you need them by putting their stickers above your bed or your desk, in your notebooks, etc.

As _____ as a
stag

As **strong** as a bear

As _____ as a
dog

66

As _____ as
an elephant

As _____ as a
bird

As _____ as a
leopard

As _____ as a
dolphin

As _____ as a
hedgehog

As _____ as a
monkey

As _____ as a
_____

Choose your own animal.
When do you
need this power?

67

The Frog's Story:
They Called Him Good-for-Nothing

THERE WAS ONCE a family of seven children. Each child had a major talent: The first could cut wood, the second was a good hunter, the third knew how to work, the fourth was an excellent cook, the fifth knew how to cut stone, the sixth sang beautifully. Only the last little one didn't know how to do anything. They called him Good-for-Nothing.

Good-for-Nothing was sad not to know how to do anything, and since he considered himself worthless, he didn't dare to try anything.

I—who never in my life met a worthless child—decided to take an interest in him. And I brought him a pencil and a drawing book. Right away he said to me: "But I don't know how to draw!" I replied: "Try. Start with a dot or a line."

Good-for-Nothing hid himself in a corner and drew lines, circles, and dots. Then little by little, he gained confidence in himself. He drew a lot, and he ended up drawing very well.

A while later, some bandits turned up in the village. They imprisoned Good-for-Nothing and his whole family. Tied up in a dungeon, his brothers and sisters cried. But Good-for-Nothing drew. He drew mice, and the mice were so well drawn that they escaped from the drawing book and began to gnaw on the ropes that held the prisoners.

When they were free, his brothers and sisters hugged and kissed Good-for-Nothing, and all of them agreed to find him a new name. They called him Can-Do-Anything!

You Are the Artist!

Starting at this dot, draw the most beautiful form you can imagine.

There's no way to succeed and no way to fail.

Here's a story that you can complete and illustrate.
Let your imagination speak.

The Story of the Cuddly Bear Who

There was once a cuddly bear who was terribly bored all the way on top of
_____ where she was waiting without moving.

This bear was very special. She was the only one who could _____
_____
_____
_____
_____

That is why the frog invited her to come to his house to give her a nice
surprise.

But the cuddly bear saw that sadness was all around _____ .
So to bring some happiness, she had the idea of _____
_____ and she asked her friend the _____
to _____
_____
_____ to help her.

And what did they do? They _____
_____
_____
_____

And that's how the cuddly bear, her friend the _____
_____ and _____
lived happily ever after!

What Do You Really Care About?

Sometimes everything is just fine as it is. But sometimes, everything goes wrong. They make fun of you in school, you get in an argument with a friend, or someone you love gets sick. There are situations that you can't change, because you are too little or because things are the way they are.

But you can do something: you can make a wishing tree.

YOUR WISHING TREE

What do you really care about? What would you like to change in yourself or in others? You're going to be able to make a wishing tree and hang it up in your room.

YOU NEED

- some little branches, some chopsticks, or some paper straws

- some thread or some string

- some clear tape

PREPARATION

1. Cut out the tree leaves and write your deepest wishes on the back.

2. Cut and hang threads of different lengths on the branches, as in the illustration, with a thread all the way on top to hang it on a wall in your room.

3. Using the tape, hang all the wishing leaves at the ends of the threads.

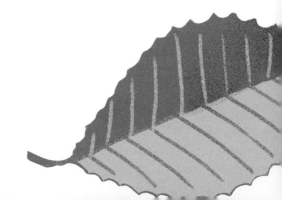

A Surprise Creation

Ask somebody to join you. You're going to draw with another person—holding on to the pencil together. Sit opposite or next to each other. Take a blank sheet of paper, and with both of you holding the pencil together, try to draw a frog. Go ahead and get started! What happens? When both of you are in charge of the pencil, and you do not know what the other person wants, you learn to "dance together."

Accepting things the way they come helps you to experience them better.

6

It's Nice to Be Kind

Kindness is one of the most important things.
Everybody can be kind. It's like a gentle rain that waters
everything. And if sometimes you're not kind,
it's important to realize it. That's the key to making peace.

Kindness touches your heart
and makes it possible for you
to grow and to have confidence
in yourself and in others.

All Hearts Are the Same Color

Every person has a heart that beats, and this heart is always the same, no matter where that person comes from.

1. Stick a heart sticker (see the end of the book) on each child's heart.

2. What part of the world is this scene happening in? Can you put the appropriate letter in each circle?

A. Latin America

B. Europe

C. Africa

D. India

E. Japan

It's Good to Love and Be Loved

1. Cut out these envelopes and love notes.

2. Fill them in by thinking about what
you love about the people around.

3. Put the note in the envelope,
which you can make as shown below.

4. You can give someone this little gift,
or put it under their pillow.

from ....

.... to

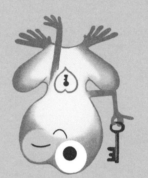

I love you because . . .

You love me because . . .

Little Kisses

from _____

to _____

This heart is for you,
because . . .

I just wanted
to tell you . . .

Little Kisses

from..........................

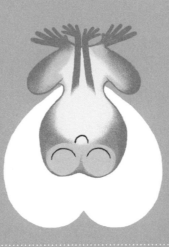

to

....

You're the best

in the world

Little Kisses

You are always so . . .

. . . .

Happiness Has a Thousand Colors

Color this rainbow with your favorite colors.

Being Happy

Happiness is knowing you're happy at the moment you're happy! Often we pay more attention to what we don't like. If we paid more attention to the nice things that happen, we'd see that there are more of them than we think.

TRACK 6

THE BIRD OF HAPPINESS

1. To end this book, you can listen to the last meditation in the audio download.

2. Now draw what you saw while flying with the bird of happiness.

Hooray! You Understand the Secret of Attention

You have done all the attention exercises very well.
Now, you have the honor of being a member of the Frog Club.

When you feel the need to be calm and attentive, you can hang this door sign on the door to your room.

Cut out this door sign and put some glue
on the back of it, and fold it in half.

Super frog

For having done all the attention exercises very well, I am now a member of the Frog Club

Your First Name and Your Signature

Signature of the Club Director

Shhhhhhhhhhhhhh!

I'm meditating!

It's Your Turn!

Each player throws the die. The first one to throw a 6 starts the game. Take turns rolling the die, and follow the instructions for the number on the square you land on. The goal is to get to the Frog Club in square 63.

5. Pick a player and whisper a compliment in her/his ear that comes from the bottom of your heart.

6. You get to throw the die two more times. How do you feel?

9. Ask somebody to stand up with you. You're going to make three funny movements: with your eyes, with your hands, and, last, with your whole body. The other person has to observe them attentively and imitate them. If they make a mistake, they have to go back three squares.

12. Close your eyes for a few seconds. Imagine that you are capable of flying anywhere. Where would you like to go? And what would you like to do there? Tell everyone this daydream.

14. Remember a moment today when you felt happy. What made you happy? Tell this story to the others.

18. Go back five squares.

19. Stay on the nearest water lily for two turns. Take advantage of this time to breathe. Feel your belly go up and down, then it will be no problem to wait. Relax!

23. The good things in life are free. Act out three things that make you happy. For example: cuddling, laughing till your stomach hurts, waking up and telling yourself you can go back to sleep.

27. Sing your favorite song and ask others to sing with you.

31. Stay on the nearest water lily until you throw a 6 with your die. Breathe and relax....

36. Look around you and find three things that are red.

41. You can throw the die again.

42. Go back four squares.

45. Long option: Get a stuffed toy. Another player puts on some music with his/her phone or tablet. The stuffed toy is passed from hand to hand, and when the music stops, the one who has the stuffed toy imitates an animal. The others have to guess what it is. The one who guesses advances 3 squares. Repeat three times.

Short option: We're happy when we do things with someone else. What would you like to do? With whom? Try to schedule that for this week.

50. Secret mission: Think of somebody you don't like very much or whom you never play with. Write that person something nice (there's something nice in each of us). When you see that person, slip her/him your little note.

52. Stay there for one turn and take advantage of it to breathe.

54. Ask each player what they like the most about you. Then tell them your favorite thing about them.

56. Put your left hand in front of you like a mirror. Spread the fingers apart. Put the index finger of your right hand at the bottom of your left thumb. Go up the length of your thumb with your finger while breathing in. When you get to the top of your thumb, breathe out till you get back down to the bottom of your thumb. Then breathe in again while going up your index finger. At the top of the index finger, the same thing, breathe out as you go down, etc. Go up and down all your fingers.

58. Stay silent for 15 seconds and listen to the sounds in the room and outside. Tell the others what you hear.

59. Fill up a glass with water, take it in your left hand, and walk all around the room without spilling a drop. You need all your attention.

63. Congratulations! Now you are part of the Frog Club!

The Big Family Frog

Game

for 2 to 4 players

YOU NEED

a pawn or
a little pebble for
each player

a die

some pieces
of paper

a pencil

a tablet or a phone
with some music

a stuffed toy or
a small pillow

Kindness is like a light rain that waters everything without leaving anything out.

In the warmth
of my opening heart,
it's nice,
I'm safe,
and everything
is fine.

Your pause button

pp. 28–29

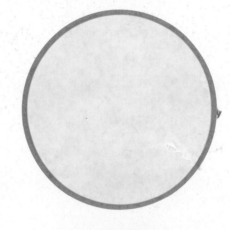

Your totem animals

pp. 66–67

They possess superpowers.
They can be helpful to you
in a bad situation.
For example, when you're
afraid and you can't fall
asleep. The sticker
of the strongest animal
can protect you.

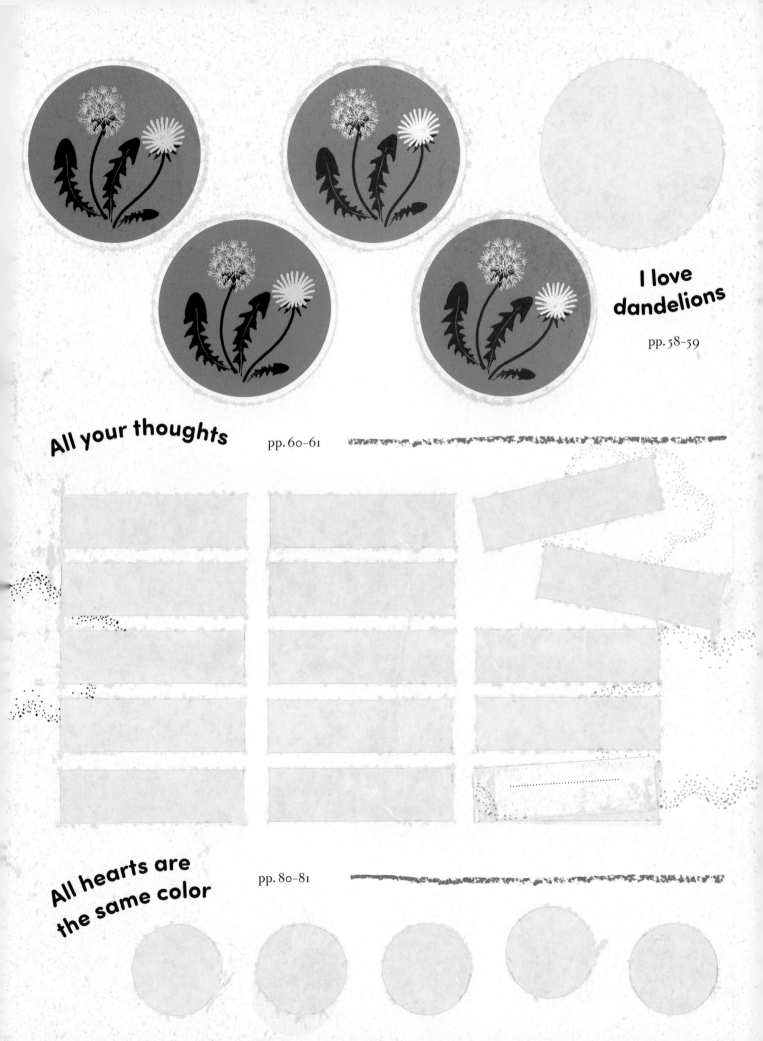

I love
dandelions

pp. 58–59

All your thoughts

pp. 60–61

All hearts are
the same color

pp. 80–81